ROCKFORD PUBLIC LIBRARY

Rockford, Illinois

www.rockfordpubliclibrary.org

815-965-9511

Virtual Apprentice

AIRLINE PILOT

By Don Rauf
and Monique Vescia

Ferguson

An imprint of Infobase Publishing

Virtual Apprentice: Airline Pilot

Ferguson
An imprint of Infobase Publishing, Inc.
132 West 31st Street
New York, NY 10001

Library of Congress Cataloging-in-Publication Data

Rauf, Don.
  Virtual apprentice. Airline pilot / Don Rauf and Monique Vescia.
    p. cm.
  Includes index.
  ISBN 978-0-8160-6755-8 (hc : alk. paper) 1.
Airplanes–Piloting–Vocational guidance–Juvenile literature. 2. Air
pilots–Juvenile literature. I. Vescia, Monique. II. Title. III. Title:
Airline pilot.
  TL561.R38 2007
  629.13023–dc22

          2006036566

Ferguson books are available at special discounts when purchased in bulk quantities for businesses, associations, institutions, or sales promotions. Please call our Special Sales Department in New York at (212) 967-8800 or (800) 322-8755.

You can find Ferguson on the World Wide Web at http://www.fergpubco.com

Produced by Bright Futures Press (http://www.brightfuturespress.com)
Series created by Diane Lindsey Reeves
Interior design by Tom Carling, carlingdesign.com
Cover design by Salvatore Luongo

Photo Credits: Table of Contents; Page 5 Eray Haciosmanoglu; Page 7 Bettmann/CORBIS; Page 8 Bettman/CORBIS; Page 11 Bettman/CORBIS; Page 15 Vera Bogaerts; Page 16 Anton Foltin; Page 19 Natthawat Wongrat; Page 22 Xavier Marchant; Page 25 Svetlana Larina; Page 26 David Hancock; Page 28 Christian Lagarek; Page 30 Scott Pehrson; Page 33 Noam Wind; Page 34 Djordje Zivaljevic; Page 39 James Leynse/CORBIS; Page 42 Brownie Harris/CORBIS.

Note to Readers: Please note that every effort was made to include accurate Web site addresses for kid-friendly resources listed throughout this book. However, Web site content and addresses change often and the author and publisher of this book cannot be held accountable for any inappropriate material that may appear on these Web sites. In the interest of keeping your on-line exploration safe and appropriate, we strongly suggest that all Internet searches be conducted under the supervision of a parent or other trusted adult.

Printed in the United States of America

Bang PKG 10 9 8 7 6 5 4 3 2 1

This book is printed on acid-free paper.

CONTENTS

Welcome to the Pilot's High-Flying World

The sky is a crowded place. More than 35,000 airplanes take off and land safely in the U.S. each day, carrying thousands of people to their destinations and back home again. More than three million people around the world fly somewhere every day. Helicopters hover over big-city highways reporting on rush-hour traffic; float planes land on lakes and taxi people across to docks. Airplanes transport tons of mail and cargo, bring smokejumpers to the sites of forest fires, and help carry wounded soldiers away from the battlefield. Every one of these aircraft, whether it's a multimillion-dollar jumbo jet, a two-seat Cessna, a Blackhawk helicopter, or an advertising blimp, is piloted by a skilled individual who has logged more than 1,000 flight hours so he or she could realize a dream as old as time: to take flight.

Nobody becomes a pilot by accident—it takes determination and hard work and an all-consuming interest in airplanes and aviation history. Were you born with your head in the clouds? Do you beg your parents to take you to air shows? Is the airport one of your favorite hangouts? Does your heart race when a jet roars by overhead? If you dream of the day you'll soar like a bird, you've come to the right book.

Virtual Apprentice: Airline Pilot puts you in the cockpit and lets you experience, firsthand, what it's like to climb a cloud-bank and get paid for doing it. What's it really like to work in an "office" that's 35,000 feet above the ground, moving forward at speeds close to 600 miles per hour? Hear what real airline pilots and other aviation professionals have to say about their jobs. Learn about the past and future of aviation, practice talking like a pilot, and challenge yourself with activities and quizzes. It's time to find out if you have what it takes to become a pilot. So buckle up—you're in for the ride of your life!

Are you ready to take off for a sky-high career?

CHAPTER 1

Up, Up, and Away

You've heard about Orville and Wilbur. But they wouldn't have gotten off the ground without their sister, Katharine. You can read about her in *The Wright Sister* by Richard Maurer (Brookfield, Conn.: Roaring Brook Press, 2003). Other sibling teams include aviation pioneers Joseph and Marvel Crosson, and Alfred, John, and Matilde Moisant (the second American woman to earn a pilot's license).

Nearly everyone imagines, at one time or another, what it would be like to fly. Maybe when you were little you, like countless other clueless kids, took a running leap off a chair, porch, or other high perch to see if you could fly like a bird. Undoubtedly, you made the same painful discovery as all the other kids when you found out that you couldn't!

Just like you, ancient humans watched birds swoop through the air and wished they could soar above the earth with that same grace and freedom. You might have heard of the ancient Greek myth of Icarus, the boy who flew using wings his father, Daedalus, built—until the hot Mediterranean sun melted the wax that held them together, and Icarus fell into the sea. Nearly every culture has its own stories and myths of flight, from winged Babylonian kings to the famous flying emperor of China. The ancient Indian epic poem, the *Mahabharata*, which dates back 2,500–3,000 years ago, includes descriptions of flying machines called *vimánas*. Some researchers wonder if such machines were actually built and flown thousands of years before the Wright brothers got airborne in 1903.

"**Aviation** is proof that, given **the will**, we have the **capacity** to achieve the **impossible.**"
—WWI FLYING ACE, EDDIE RICKENBACKER

The Wright brothers made aviation history when their homemade plane took off and stayed airborne for 12 seconds.

One thing is certain, though—the desire to fly is an aspiration shared by human beings throughout history. Given human ingenuity, it's not surprising that we eventually figured out how to make that dream a reality.

Defying Gravity

Leonardo da Vinci was always a close observer of nature. About 500 years ago, this Italian artist and inventor studied the way birds flap their wings in flight and designed a variety of machines to imitate those movements and, with luck, allow a human to fly. Da Vinci's designs were never air-tested, but his ideas influenced

The infamous Hindenburg, one of the largest aircraft ever built, flies over Manhattan.

others. However, early attempts to imitate birds by constructing wings and trying to flap them fast enough to stay aloft were a big flop—literally! The first real breakthrough in human aviation came when people figured out that they could fill balloons and other constructions with lighter-than-air gases such as hydrogen and helium. In 1783, the Montgolfier brothers of France (one of many sibling teams in aviation history) successfully launched the world's first passenger balloon. Filled with a mixture of very dense and stinky smoke made from wool, straw, and old shoes, the balloon stayed aloft for almost half an hour, landing six miles away.

The trouble with those early hot-air balloons is that there was no way to steer them—they had to go where the wind pushed them. That problem was solved in the construction of the dirigible, which means "steerable." Developed in the late 1920s, the cigar-shaped hydrogen-filled dirigible featured propellers and a rudder for steering. These whales of the air were not exactly lightning-fast, though—the German-made Graf Zeppelin, the first airship to make a successful transatlantic flight, had a top speed of just 18 miles per hour. Over time dirigibles improved, making regular trips at 68 miles per hour. Passenger airships like the Graf Zeppelin offered a luxurious way to travel. Elegant dinners were prepared by chefs and served on fine china; there were private showers in the staterooms, and unbeatable views. But the age of passenger airships came to an abrupt and terrible end when the *Hindenburg*, the largest airship ever built, burst into flames while docking at Lakehurst, New Jersey, in 1937. Thirty-six of the 97 passengers and crew onboard died, mostly from injuries sustained jumping from the burning aircraft. After that, people didn't want to travel by dirigible anymore.

Pioneers of Powered Flight

In the 1890s, Otto Lilienthal of Germany built and flew some of the first hang gliders. An American named Samuel Langley and Frenchman, Clément Ader, each built steam-powered flying machines, but—big problem—these crafts could not be controlled once they were airborne. The real challenge for early inventors was to design a machine that could take off, be flown in a controlled way, and safely landed. Over a century ago, on December

CHECK IT OUT

If you go to Moffett Field, near San Jose, California, you can see the giant hangar that housed these enormous airships, relatives of the colorful blimps you'll see hovering over baseball stadiums today, or you can see images of this humongous hangar at http://www.moffettfieldmuseum.org.

17, 1903, Orville and Wilbur Wright, two bicycle repairmen from Dayton, Ohio, flew into aviation history. With Wilbur piloting the craft, the *Kitty Hawk Flyer* was launched from a sand dune called Kill Devil Hill on the windy Outer Banks of North Carolina. On its initial launch, the *Flyer* only stayed aloft for 12 seconds and traveled 120 feet. Still, it represented the first powered flight with a pilot aboard in a heavier-than-air machine, the precursor to all air travel to follow. This historic event is featured on the North Carolina state quarter, issued in 2001.

Lift, Weight, Thrust, and Drag

The mechanics of flight depends on four little words: *lift, weight, thrust,* and *drag.* For an airplane to fly straight and level, the amount of lift must be equal to the weight of the aircraft, and the amount of thrust must be equal to the amount of drag. Airplanes create thrust using propellers, jet engines, or rockets. When you stick your hand out the window of a moving car you feel drag— the resistance an object encounters as it moves through a fluid like air (yes, air is a fluid) or water. When you and a friend are racing your bikes, you bend forward over your handlebars to decrease drag, so you can move faster. Airplanes are designed to reduce drag, so they will need less fuel to get where they're going.

The average 747 loaded with passengers and baggage weighs a ton—or, to be more accurate, 435 tons (870,000 pounds)! How does something that heavy manage to get off the ground? The answer is lift, the aerodynamic force that is created by a plane's wings. If an airplane can move forward at sufficient speed, and its wings are wide enough, the air will lift it up.

Setting Records and Taking Risks

From the early days of aviation, pilots had to figure out how these four forces worked and how to use them to their advantage. Much like the Wright brothers, many early

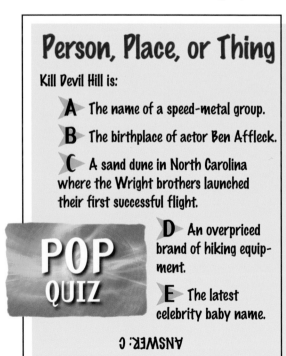

Person, Place, or Thing

Kill Devil Hill is:

A The name of a speed-metal group.

B The birthplace of actor Ben Affleck.

C A sand dune in North Carolina where the Wright brothers launched their first successful flight.

D An overpriced brand of hiking equipment.

E The latest celebrity baby name.

ANSWER: C

POP QUIZ

pilots were inventors, whose growing understanding of aerodynamics helped them to design and build better airplanes. They set out to test the limits of this new form of transportation and find out who could fly farthest and fastest.

In 1927, Charles Lindbergh flew his plane, *The Spirit of St. Louis,* nonstop across the Atlantic Ocean from New York to Paris. During the nearly 34-hour solo flight, Lindbergh kept himself awake by sticking his head out of the plane's open window. Five years later, Amelia Earhart became the first woman pilot to make a transatlantic solo flight. She was also the first person to fly alone across the Pacific Ocean from Honolulu, Hawaii, to Oakland, California.

Flying Circuses

Some early pilots were also entertainers, whose shows and stunts dazzled the crowds who assembled on fairgrounds and in cow pastures to watch them. These

Amelia Earhart met a mysterious end when attempting to fly around the world in 1937.

pilots were called *barnstormers* because they often paid farmers for permission to land planes in their fields. Bessie Coleman, the first African-American woman pilot, was a barnstormer who thrilled witnesses with her death-defying air stunts. Barnstormers flew planes upside down, looped the loop, performed "death drops," dangled from trapezes in flight, and jumped midair from one plane to another!

War Birds

It didn't take people long to realize the advantages of airplanes in an armed conflict: Airplanes could be used to gather information—such as in aerial photographs—and they could also drop bombs. The side with the most air power could control the skies and win the war. War increased production of airplanes, spurred new designs, and the aeronautics industry grew by leaps and bounds. During World War I (1914–1918), the average flying speed increased from 50 mph to 125 mph. During World War II (1939–1945), pilots flew huge bomber planes like the B-17 "Flying Fortress."

The most daring and successful pilots in wartime were known as flying aces if they racked up more than five victories during "dogfights"–aerial battles between planes. Piloting military planes is an incredibly dangerous job; during World War I, poorly made aircraft sometimes broke apart in midair, pilots were not equipped with parachutes, and their wooden-and-canvas planes often caught fire during combat. During both world wars, male and female pilots risked their lives. The WASPs–an acronym for the Women Airforce Service Pilots who flew during WWII–had lower accident rates than male pilots.

A surplus of planes after World War I enabled the growth of the airline passenger industry. Some of the first commercial passenger planes were converted bombers, which could carry 11 peo-

Fear Factor

An airplane cockpit is a small space, with even less legroom than a cramped office cubicle. Do you feel panicky in tight places? Here's how to find out if this aspect of a pilot's job would drive you nuts.

You're riding alone in an elevator that gets stuck between floors. Do you:

A Pull out your cell phone and start playing the mini video game that's on it?

B Picture the walls closing in and try your best not to freak out?

C Start jumping up and down to get the darn thing moving again?

If you chose B and your palms get sweaty just thinking about elevators, you may not be comfortable in an airplane cockpit. Since you prefer the wide-open spaces, you could always train to be a member of the ground crew.

ple from Paris to London. (Today's jumbo jets can carry about 400 passengers.) Jet engines were introduced toward the end of WWII to replace propellers. The first pilot to fly faster than the speed of sound was Charles "Chuck" Yeager, a World War II ace and test pilot who flew military jets. Yeager broke the sound barrier on October 14, 1947, which caused a sonic boom. (The nose of a plane flying at supersonic speeds creates a shock wave that makes a loud bang that is called a sonic boom.) Military test pilots, such as John Glenn (the first human to orbit Earth in a spacecraft), joined the space program and became the first astronauts.

To Infinity...and Beyond

In just over 100 years, aviation has gone from a daring experiment to a fact of daily life that most of us take for granted. In the not-too-distant future, people may ride in rocket-powered airplanes that travel from one coast of the United States to the other in 30 minutes. Space shuttles may regularly fly sightseers into space and around the moon. And you might be the pilot at the controls of one of these incredible new flying machines. As famous World War I flying ace Eddie Rickenbacker once said, "Aviation is proof that, given the will, we have the capacity to achieve the impossible."

CHECK IT OUT

You can learn lots more about the life of famous aviator Charles Lindbergh at http://www.charleslindbergh.com. This site includes details about Lindbergh's historic transatlantic flight and lots of other fascinating stuff about this complex American hero.

CHAPTER 2

Pilots on the Job

People fly so much nowadays it can seem pretty routine. But if you take the time to look out your window when you're soaring high over the earth, you can still feel a little thrill no matter how often you fly. You're gliding through the clouds, looking down at rivers, mountains, and neighborhoods as you speed to your destination. For pilots, the excitement comes from actually commanding an aircraft that is giving their passengers the ability to fly! Pilots have mastered this amazing skill, and many will tell you that it can still be exhilarating years after learning how to do it.

Many pilots have performed hundreds if not thousands of flights, and although they may make it look easy, getting a plane safely from point A to point B requires a lot of training. When people think of pilots, those who fly commercial passenger jets often come to mind. But pilots fly many different types of planes for many different purposes.

Schedules for pilots can be crazy. Flights often leave early in the morning or late at night, and they have to arrive at least an hour before takeoff to prepare. On the plus side, they can work as few as eight days in a month to as many as 20. At a major airline, a typical work schedule is about 14 days in a month.

FUN FACTOID

Famous pilot Amelia Earhart built her own roller coaster before she was 10 years old.

> "The way I see it, you can either work for a living or you can fly airplanes. Me, I'd rather fly."
>
> —LEN MORGAN, FORMER AIRLINE CAPTAIN

Pilots don't take their work home with them, either. When they're done with their flight schedule, they can leave work behind. Of course, they have to be away from home and family a lot, which can be tough. They might spend half a month or more away from home living out of a suitcase in a hotel room or in a "crash pad" with other pilots. Naturally, pilots are experts at packing suitcases because they do it all the time.

What about you? Do you think you'd make a good pilot? Put yourself in a pilot's cockpit and see how you like it.

Pack, Prepare, Get Ready to Soar

Imagine this. Your alarm goes off at 4:00 a.m. as you wake up to your first day as a commercial airline pilot! You jump out of bed, shower, and put on your uniform—a clean, pressed collared shirt, a winged name badge, simple dark slacks, and your captain's hat and jacket. (Your jacket features four stripes on the sleeve because you're the captain. The first officer's coat has three stripes.)

You grab your suitcase, which you packed the night before with enough clothes to last five days away from home.

Pilots check in with the air traffic control tower before taking off, during flights, and when landing.

15

Don't forget your cell phone and laptop so you can keep up with activities at home and any other work you may have. Finally, you take your flight bag, which is stuffed with essentials—your flight operations manual with all the procedures you must follow, navigation charts, a flashlight, and your earpiece to hear air traffic controllers. Although your first flight leaves at 7:00 a.m., you have to give yourself time to prepare, so you want to arrive at the terminal by 6:00 a.m. to do all your prep work.

While many people commute by car to their jobs, pilots often travel by plane to theirs. To drive from your home to your base airport or "domicile" would take several hours, but it's only a 45-minute plane ride. Airlines have arrangements with one another to let airline staff travel to work for free. Seats for airline personnel are called jumpseats and they're unavailable if a flight is completely full of paying passengers. Fortunately, the flight you need has a free seat available, and you basically hitch a ride to work,

Just another day at the office?

Aviation Mysteries

Occasionally pilots fly off into the wild blue yonder and never return. Attempting to fly around the world, Amelia Earhart and her navigator, Fred Noonan, set out from Lau, New Guinea, on July 2, 1937, and disappeared forever. In 1945, an entire squadron of bomber planes vanished, in peacetime and fair weather, during a routine training flight off the coast of Florida in the Bermuda Triangle; not a single one of the five planes or the 14 crewmen of Flight 19 has ever been found. Antoine de Saint-Exupery, a famous French pilot and author of *The Little Prince*, set off on a spying mission during World War II and never returned. This last mystery was finally solved in 2004, when the wreckage of Saint-Exupery's plane was discovered on the seafloor near the south of France. Search the Web using the keywords "aviation mysteries" and make a list of the 10 most tantalizing cases of all time.

a practice known in the airline business as "deadheading." You arrive at 5:45 a.m., walk through security, and go immediately to the pilot lounge (officially called "flight operations") in time for "sign in." You find an empty computer in the lounge and print out the details of your flight—weather conditions, maintenance status of your plane, a list of who you will be flying with. You also check your mailbox for updates to your flight manual and other airline news.

Now it's time to meet the rest of your crew and check over your aircraft. You head through another security gate where an agent checks your identification, and you greet the flight attendants, who are already aboard preparing the coffee and readying the cabin. In the cockpit, you say hello to your copilot and discuss procedures. You also "build your nest," which is pilot slang for preparing your spot—tucking away your flight bag, displaying your airway charts and checklists, and plugging in your headset. Because you're the captain, your seat is always on the left; the copilot sits on the right. You check all the panels and gauges to make sure they are working correctly. A computerized checklist

POP QUIZ

Match the Pilots to Their Planes

When you think of pilots you might first picture those who fly for commercial airlines, but pilots can specialize in a lot of other areas. Match the type of pilot with the type of work they do and you'll see how diverse pilots' jobs can be.

1 Air Taxi Pilot

2 Cargo Pilot

3 Air Ambulance Pilot

4 Crop Duster

5 Test Pilot

6 Helicopter Pilot

7 Military Pilot

8 Skywriter

9 Corporate Jet Pilot

10 Stunt Pilot

11 Aerial Photography Pilot

A Hurries patients requiring medical attention to the best hospitals or other facilities.

B Commands "microjets" that bypass the crowds of airports and flies private passengers quickly to their destination.

C Specializes in flights that help capture photos from high in an airplane, often for geographic purposes.

D Delivers packages and materials. Many work for big delivery services such as Federal Express and UPS.

E Transports business executives in the company's own private aircraft to get them to meetings around the country.

F Operates small planes that spray large fields of vegetables and grains with insecticide. The key is to fly low and slow.

G Flies at low altitudes for jobs such as traffic reporting, rescue, medical emergencies, and police work.

H Carries out operations for the Air Force and Navy for national defense. These military men and women may fly cargo, passengers, or engage in combat.

I Spells out advertising messages in the sky using letters that are 2,400 feet tall using a special smoke that is actually liquid paraffin wax.

J Works for movies or air shows doing trick maneuvers. You need to be a bit of a daredevil to take on this job.

K Flies new or modified planes to see if they can safely fly and operate the way they are intended to.

ANSWERS: 1-B, 2-D, 3-A, 4-F, 5-K, 6-G, 7-H, 8-I, 9-E, 10-J, 11-C

appears on a screen to make sure you don't miss anything. You're all fueled up and all other systems are ready to go.

With things all set in the cockpit, you head down to the tarmac to examine the outside of the plane. This is called the "preflight." You check the tires and look for damage on the body of the plane. You examine the blades in the engine. In cold weather, ice can accumulate on them or the plane may have ingested a bird, and that can do a lot of damage. If there's any sign of trouble, you immediately get a maintenance crew member to investigate.

Back in the cockpit, you and the copilot do a final check, making sure all luggage and passengers are onboard. You're concerned with how people and luggage are placed in the plane because the balance is key to a successful flight. You also get an up-to-date weather report. Weather is a big concern for you because it will determine your route, the height you fly at (altitude), and the speed at which you travel for the safest trip possible.

Ready and waiting for take off.

All Systems Go

Attendants secure all doors, and now you're ready for pushback. After disconnecting the plane from the external air conditioning and electric of the terminal, a special vehicle called "the tug" pushes the plane away from the gate so you can get to the runway.

You start the engines and communicate with the air traffic controllers who handle ramp and ground control. You taxi out to the runway and the control tower tells you how many planes are ahead of you and when you should take off. You are in constant contact with air traffic controllers throughout your flight to make sure you are coordinating with other planes and their flight paths.

Takeoff and landing are the hardest parts of flying, so as you take off you're extra alert to details. You and your copilot are watching the engine gauges—how fast blades are turning, oil temperature, and pressure. Brakes are off. Lights are on. You're cleared for takeoff. You hit V1 speed, about 160 miles per hour. That's the speed you need to takeoff. You lift the nose of the plane

Bull's-eye!

As the famous aviator Charles Lindbergh once said, "In my profession life itself depends on accuracy." There is no margin for error when you're flying a plane. If you're a commercial airline pilot, the lives of hundreds of people depend on you, and a single mistake could be fatal. Are you a detail-oriented person? Do you automatically double- and triple-check your work? Fill in the blanks to find out.

When I finish a writing assignment for class, I always _____.

Before I jump on my bike and ride to my best friend's house, I put on _____.

The inside of my bedroom closet most resembles _____.

When my teacher asks us to team up with other students on a class project, I am the person who _____.

If you never bother reading over your class assignments to check for errors, you put on your iPod instead of a helmet when you're biking, and your closet looks like an explosion in a sock factory, you might want to get your act together before heading off to test your wings.

True or False?

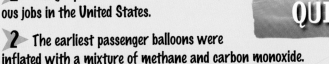
POP
QUIZ

1 Being a pilot is one of the most dangerous jobs in the United States.

2 The earliest passenger balloons were inflated with a mixture of methane and carbon monoxide.

3 During World War I, pilots were not equipped with parachutes.

4 The four aerodynamic forces that make flight possible are weight, drag, thrust, and hope.

5 Most pilots like to change airlines every few years to improve their salaries.

ANSWERS:

1. True. While pilot is currently ranked as the third most dangerous profession in the U.S., pilots who fly crop dusters or work as bush pilots, flying small planes into remote areas, have a much higher accident rate than commercial airline pilots.

2. False. The first balloons were filled with hot smoke created by burning garbage.

3. True. Parachutes were first considered unnecessary weight and did not become standard equipment for American military pilots until after World War I.

4. False. That last one should be lift.

5. False. The majority of commercial airline pilots prefer to work for a single airline for the duration of their careers. If they change airlines, pilots lose their seniority—and all the good stuff that comes with it.

and you increase speed to V2, which is what you need to "climb out." You retract the wheels so there is less drag. You continue to climb until you are at cruising speed (about 550 mph) and cruising altitude, which is anywhere between 29,000 and 40,000 feet. Flying so high is very efficient for your airplane. The air is less dense so it's easier to fly faster and the air is colder high up, which helps your engines to combust more efficiently.

Cruising Along at 35,000 Feet

At cruising altitude you hook the plane into autopilot and relax a bit. The plane automatically follows the designated route or highway in the sky. Just like some automobile drivers rely on a satellite global positioning system (GPS) to guide them, so does your plane. You'll send a message to your destination estimating your time of arrival. Throughout the trip, you scan the panel to check the fuel supply, engine conditions, air conditioning, and hydraulics. You can keep an eye out the window, too, for any other air traffic.

About two hours into the flight, you hit some turbulence because of some bad weather conditions, so you get on the speaker to assure your passengers. "Ladies and gentlemen, this is your captain," you say with calmness and authority. "Due to some thunderstorm activity we may experience a few bumps for the next five minutes. Please keep your seatbelts fastened."

When you hit a patch of turbulence, you contact air traffic controllers, who can direct you to a new altitude where the turbulence will be less or where you might catch a tailwind that will speed your trip and save you fuel.

Pilot on the left, copilot on the right equals cockpit teamwork.

Coming Down to Earth

After your five-hour flight from California to New York, you start your descent to land. It's a bit foggy, so you turn to your instrument panel to guide you when there's poor visibility. Another option when visibility is limited is to set the plane to do an automatic landing, but conditions improve, so you decide to land on your own.

You reduce engine power and speed and adjust your wing flaps to slow down. You follow a "glide path" down and eventually lower your landing gear. You land at about 120 mph. Using foot controls, you activate the brakes, but you need to reverse thrust of the engine as well and raise a set of panels on the wings called "spoilers," which increase wind resistance so you can slow down.

Then you taxi to a gate so passengers can "deplane" as fast as possible. You, too, are eager to get off. You have about an hour before you change to another plane and head out again. Even though you're not hungry, you decide to grab a sandwich and eat because judging from your schedule you may not have another break until late at night. You also drink a lot of water–it's so easy to dehydrate on a plane because the air is very dry. All too quickly, your hour is up, and you're going through takeoff again. When you finally land for the night, you look forward to heading to the hotel and your 12 hours off until the next day. You couldn't fly sooner if you wanted to. Pilots are required to rest a set amount of hours–they're not legal to fly unless they do.

Before you know it though, your alarm is ringing and it's up, up, and away again.

Get Some Air

If you're interested in planes but you've never had the chance to fly in one, you should definitely check out the EAA (Experimental Aviation Association) Young Eagles Program. Launched in 1992, this program offers kids ages 8–17 a chance to fly free in a general aviation airplane. (For info visit http://www.youngeagles.org.) The chairman of Young Eagles is actor Harrison Ford, who—besides being a big-shot movie star (in *Star Wars* and the Indiana Jones films)—is also an experienced pilot.

FIND OUT MORE

CHAPTER 3

Aviation Tech and Trends

Next time you fly somewhere, take a peek into the cockpit as you struggle on board with all your carry-ons. You'll see the pilot's workspace: a small window and a sea of dials, knobs, switches, and gauges. Pilots have to know how all these instruments function. The altimeter, which measures the altitude or height of the plane, is one of the gauges. The artificial horizon gauge shows the angle of the plane and the directional gyroscope indicates if the plane is flying straight.

All these controls represent advances in technology that have made air travel safer and faster. A look back at some of the major technological landmarks in aviation over the past 70 years shows you how much air travel has improved.

Jet Engines

Without the jet engine, plane travel would be pretty slow. A jet engine produces a high-speed exhaust through a type of gas turbine engine. The first jet engine plane was flown in the 1930s, and by 1949 the first commercial jet airliner took off, starting the era of speedy air travel. Advances in technology made the jet engine increasingly more powerful. Chuck

FUN FACTOID

Better hold it! Bathrooms only became standard on aircraft five years after the first commercial passenger plane began flying in 1914.

Yeager flew a jet faster than the speed of sound, and the Concorde, the first commercial supersonic jet, carried passengers from New York to Paris in about three hours. It was grounded in 2003 for financial reasons.

Cabin Pressurization

Above 10,000 feet, natural air pressure is too low for people to absorb oxygen in a natural way. That's why the first commercial pilots, who flew unpressurized planes like the Boeing 247 and DC3, had to keep them flying no higher than 10,000 feet or passengers would get dizzy and even faint. At 10,000 feet, turbulence is a problem as well, and as a result, motion sickness was a lot more common. (Still, the plastic-lined air sickness bag—commonly known as the barf bag—wasn't invented until 1949!)

Boeing had a breakthrough in the 1940s when it introduced the Stratoliner, a commercial aircraft that was pressurized. An air compressor pumped air into the cabin to increase the pressure so planes could fly much higher. Since jet planes fly faster and more efficiently at higher altitudes, pressurization was a real turning point for the airline industry. As a result, you can

Flying is fast and fancy with elite pilots like these.

now use that barf bag as a hand puppet to amuse the toddler who has been crying the whole trip.

Computers

Before the first commercially available computers came along in the 1940s, the aircraft industry relied on humans to crunch numbers, digest data, and come up with the calculations needed to design, build, and fly planes. Pilots used special slide rules to calculate how to navigate through the air. As computers developed, aerospace engineers used the technology to develop jet engines and faster, more aerodynamic planes. By the 1950s, the integrated circuit (known today as the silicon chip) replaced the heavy tubes, and suddenly computers were getting smaller, which meant computer technology could be brought onboard a plane. Among other things, computer chips led to the development of automatic pilots, guidance systems, and safety checks.

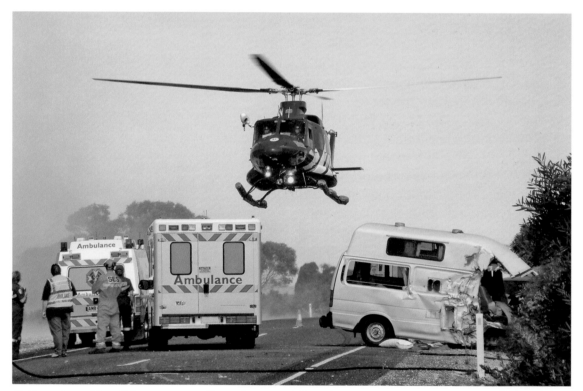

Helicopters like this one save lives by providing fast access to medical services.

Are We There Yet?

Even though modern pilots have lots of nifty devices to help them find their way in the air, sometimes they have to rely on their own navigational skills—reading maps and looking for landmarks—to guide them to their destination. Let's say that destination is your home. (What? You don't have a landing strip in your backyard? Don't worry. The pilot can park out front.) Draw a rough map of your neighborhood showing your home and at least five local landmarks that would help the pilot locate you. Show your map to friends or family. If they can instantly identify the landmarks and your home, you're heading in the right direction as far as building the navigational skills that pilots depend on.

REALITY CHECK

Radar (Radio Detection and Ranging)

On June 30, 1956, one of the most dramatic accidents in aviation history happened when two planes collided over the Grand Canyon, killing 128 people. Air traffic controllers at that time tracked planes as they radioed in their position and altitude. There was no nationwide radar, a system that uses radar waves to detect distant objects. Controllers would follow planes on paper or by moving little markers across maps. After that accident, the government passed a law that rapidly modernized air traffic control and made radar scopes a mandatory part of tracking U.S. planes. Because of radar, air traffic control is much more accurate now and midair collisions are very rare.

Global Positioning System

Global positioning systems (GPS) are an aerospace technology that uses satellites and ground controls to help pilots navigate through the sky. Some drivers of newer cars use similar systems to find directions. There are at least 24 operational GPS satellites at all times, all operated by the U.S. Air Force. GPS allows pilots and air traffic controllers to know the exact position and speed of planes. GPS is slowly replacing radar and some day soon will

Thanks to cargo planes like this, the world has become a smaller place to conduct business.

provide air traffic controllers with more accurate information to keep aircraft safely separated in the sky and on the runways.

Simulators

Flight simulators use computer game technology to re-create what it's like to take off in a plane, hit cruising altitude, and land the aircraft. Surround screens and authentic audio make learning to fly with simulations more realistic and can help fledgling pilots gain confidence without leaving the ground. Even pilots with lots of experience are required to spend time training on simulators to keep their skills sharp and up-to-date.

Enhanced Ground Proximity Warning System

One of the most important computerized inventions is called the "Enhanced Ground Proximity Warning System." This device warns pilots that they are too close to the land or water. For example, in January 2002, a Boeing 737 was making a routine landing into Tucson, Arizona, on a clear night. They mistakenly descended to 4,000 feet with a 4,687-foot mountain in front of them. With seconds away from a collision, a mechanical voice sounded in the cockpit: "Terrain! Terrain! Pull up! Pull up!" Just in time, the pilot pulled up, cleared the mountain, and landed safely. Technology saved the day!

Flight Plan for the Future

Aeronautics, the science of aviation, has evolved at supersonic speed. It's a cliché in the airline business that "The future of aviation is the next 30 seconds—long-term planning is an hour and a half." Already in development are planes that use vertical takeoff and landing (VTOL) technology and computerized "smart" wings, which respond on their own to changing flight conditions.

Air Traffic Jams? One day, you might need a pilot's license just to borrow your mom's car. The folks who brought you the

Airport ABCs

Pilots and aviation officials use a system of three-letter airport codes to identify different airports around the world. Can you match the locations of these airports with their codes?

A Fresno, California   **1** CAI

B New York (Kennedy)   **2** LAX

C Cairo, Egypt   **3** PNH

D Shannon, Ireland   **4** SNN

E Los Angeles, California   **5** FAT

F Phnom Penh, Cambodia   **6** JFK

POP QUIZ

Learn all about the history of airport codes and how the system works at this Web site: http://www.skygod.com/asstd/abc.html

ANSWERS: A-5, B-6, C-1, D-4, E-2, F-3

After the terrorist attacks on 9/11, airport screening like this became even more important.

Cars and planes are more similar than you might think. Write a list of the features you would expect these two kinds of vehicles to share. Then visit General Aviation's cool site that compares a minivan and a private plane: http://www.gaservingamerica.org/how_work/work_aircraft.htm.

moon landing and the space shuttle are currently developing carsthat both drive and fly! NASA's PAVE (Personal Air Vehicle Exploration) program hopes to have a demonstration model of its TailFan flying car ready by 2009. These "roadable air vehicles" are designed with folding wings so they'll fit into a garage. Just remember to put the top up before you take off!

The Ecofriendly Skies As the skyrocketing cost of oil and worries about global warming continue to make headlines, airlines are aggressively seeking ways to reduce the environmental impact and fuel consumption of their aircraft. As reported in the *Wall Street Journal*, in 2006, Alaska Airlines reported that it had saved $10,000 a year in fuel by taking five magazines off each plane. If you travel on that airline you'll have to pack your own *Mad* magazine!

SuperDUPERsonic Planes The airplane of the future has a funny name: scramjet. The name, which stands for Supersonic Combustion Ramjet, uses a brand-new kind of technology: The oxygen that the aircraft's engine needs to combust is drawn from the surrounding atmosphere instead of from a storage tank on board the vehicle. This means the plane can be lighter and faster. How much faster? Try 15 times the speed of sound! That means that a scramjet could travel from Tokyo to New York (currently a butt-numbing 18-hour flight) in just two hours.

Standing Room Only? If you've flown anywhere recently, you know how crowded planes have become. If the person in front of you reclines a fraction of an inch, you get pinned between your tray table and seat back! In 2003, Airbus, an aircraft manufacturer, proposed that planes be built to accommodate standing passengers for short trips, squeezing in even more paying customers per flight. So far no airlines have embraced this idea, but who knows what discomforts the future holds!

A New Space Race In 1996, a national competition called the Ansari X-Prize was announced when entrepreneur Peter Diamandis offered a $10 million prize to the first team to build a spacecraft and fly three people to an altitude of 100 kilometers (just over 62 miles). The winning entry was SpaceShipOne, designed by Burt Rutan and funded by Microsoft billionaire Paul Allen. On June 21, 2004, with pilot Mike Melvill at the controls, SpaceShipOne became the first manned private aircraft to soar into space. During the flight, Melvill opened a bag of M&Ms and watched in amazement as they floated around the cockpit.

What other amazing developments are on the aviation horizon? Will planes fly themselves one day, leaving pilots free to nap and play Sudoko during the one-hour flight from Biloxi to Moscow? Will every home have a heliport on the roof, and will kids travel to school in air taxis? Will everybody have their own personal jetpacks for buzzing around town? (We hope so!) Take a wild guess about the future of aviation—and you just might be right on target!

You can see videos taken from SpaceShipOne at http://channelev ents.aol.com/re search/xprize/index .adp.

CHAPTER 4

Pilot in Training

A lot of young people are natural thrill-seekers with a built-in urge to defy gravity. Some take flight on their skateboards, getting airborne as they soar out of the skate bowl to complete a 180-degree turn. Others fly off ramps as they tear through muddy trails on their cross-country bikes. Avid young skiers often seek out the largest moguls so they can catch air as they bullet downhill. If you're someone who likes to get your feet way off the ground and taste adventure, then becoming a pilot might be a good career choice.

Many pilots have a sports background because team sports prepare people to make quick decisions. Just like the quarterback who has to make the best play under stressful conditions, the pilot has to think fast to ensure that all the equipment is operating properly as the plane speeds to takeoff or glides to a landing. If something isn't working right on a plane, the pilot relies on snap problem-solving skills. It takes a sharp mind to handle all the elements involved with flying. Study-wise, future pilots are smart to bone up on physics, mathematics, and geography. They have to be in good physical shape, too. Captains need to pass a physical once every six months. And, as with sports, they have to know how to work with a team.

CHECK IT OUT

For information on what you need to earn your first flying license go online to http://www.soyouwanna.com.

"Aviation in itself is not inherently dangerous. But to an even greater degree than the sea, it is terribly unforgiving of any carelessness, incapacity, or neglect."

—Captain A. G. Lamplugh

Many pilots learn how to fly in the military.

The cockpit is one of the most important classrooms for pilots.

The copilot, flight attendants, mechanics, and air traffic controllers are all essential to getting passengers safely to their intended destinations.

Pilots don't fit the mold of those who want a conventional nine-to-five life. They would rather work crazy hours than be trapped in an office cubicle. They're always ready for the adventure, to meet new people, and travel to different cities. If this all sounds like you, you may have the makings of a great pilot.

Early Birds Get the Worm

If a career in aviation is at all on your radar, one of the most obvious questions to ask is: "Do you like flying?" If you've never flown before, take a flight. A beginner's ride in a small airplane is an especially good test because you can really feel what it's like to control an aircraft. The Young Eagles Program provides free flights for kids ages eight to 17. Even at a young age, you can usually arrange for an introductory flight at your local airport. Start to read up on flying to find out how planes operate and what a pilot's life is like. You can find plenty of aviation sites on the Web.

Building motorized model planes can help you gain a better understanding of the science of flight. If you get serious about flying at an early age, you might want to see if there is an aviation high school near you. Seattle, New York City, and Cleveland are among the major cities that have these specialized schools. Check out what an aviation high school is like at http://www.aviationhs.org.

Becoming a captain on a commercial airline requires a lot of training and experience. The earlier you start learning, the better.

Taking Flight

A first step in an aviation career is earning a private pilot's license, which will allow you to fly a single-engine airplane under visual flight rules (VFR), meaning visibility of at least three miles, even at night. According to FAA rules, to get a pilot's license you must be at least 16 years old, in good health, and fluent in English (the international language of aviation). For training, you have to log at least 40 hours of flying time and put in time studying to pass an FAA written test. Flight lessons are available at airports and aviation schools, and the total cost ranges between $3,000 and $5,000. If you take a very intensive course, you can earn this license in two weeks. Most students tend to go part time and earn the license over the course of three to six months.

Weather Watcher

Pilots always keep an eye on the weather. Thunderstorms and high winds can change the route a pilot flies. Heavy fog can keep a plane from landing. A future pilot should have an interest in meteorology, which is the science of weather and weather forecasting. Do you? Try some simple weather experiments to find out:

REALITY
CHECK

▶ **BUILD A BAROMETER** Barometers measure air pressure. When pressure increases, clear weather usually is coming. When pressure decreases, a storm usually is coming. You can build your own barometer by securing plastic wrap tightly on the top of an empty coffee can with a rubber band. Tape a straw to the center of the plastic wrap so about a third of the straw hangs over the edge. Tape an index card to the can behind the straw so you can mark where it is. High pressure will make the plastic wrap cave in and the straw go up, meaning clear weather. Low pressure makes the wrap puff up and the straw go down, meaning rainy weather is coming.

▶ **MAKE AN ANEMOMETER** Anemometers measure how fast the wind is blowing. A pinwheel is a type of anemometer. You can easily make one. The science project Web site at http://www.energyquest.ca.gov/projects/anemometer.html shows you how. Staple four mini paper or plastic cups facing opposite directions to the end of two sturdy 12-inch cardboard strips. Make a cross with the cardboard strips, securing them together with staples or tape. Get a pencil with a new eraser. Push a pin through the very center of the cardboard and into the eraser so when the wind blows the cups spin freely. Put the point end of the pencil in the ground and see how fast the cups spins.

FIND OUT MORE

Equal Air Time

The FAA (Federal Aviation Administration) estimates that as of the end of 2005 there were over 600,000 active pilots, but only six percent of these were women. There are plenty of famous women pilots in the history of aviation, both in civilian life and the military. Why aren't more women flying today? Come up with your own ideas, and then do some research in your school library or on the Web at home to find out what others say about why there aren't more women in the cockpit.

Once you have a private license, you can start putting in the hours and study toward higher levels of certificates, such as

• A commercial certificate that allows you to get paid for flying a plane

• A flight instructor certificate that allows you to teach others

• An airline transport certificate that allows you to fly an airliner

As you gain experience and additional training, you add "ratings" to your license. Ratings certify that you are qualified to handle different equipment. You can earn a rating to pilot multiengine airplanes, navigate by instruments during bad weather, or fly special aircraft like seaplanes, gliders, helicopters, and balloons.

Earning Your Wings

To become an airline pilot, you have to be at least 23 years old and your flight time must be at least 1,500 hours. Again, you have to pass a medical exam and prove that you have 20/20 vision (with or without glasses), good hearing, and no handicaps that would impair your performance. You also have to pass the FAA's written and flight exams. Individual airlines may have their own psychological and aptitude test that you'll have to pass.

To gain all the training necessary, pilots enroll in a flight school or join the military. Pilots in the Air Force, Navy, Marines, Coast Guard, and Army can gain a lot of flying experience and steadily build the flying hours needed. They often have the opportunity to fly different aircraft, from helicopters to jets. In return for the training, these budding pilots commit to serve their country for a set number of years (typically eight) and then, if they choose, they can pursue jobs with the airlines.

Flight schools are another training option. There are about 600 civilian flight schools in the country, including colleges and universities that offer degree-credit for pilot training. No matter what educational route you take, you should earn a college degree—most major airlines prefer these graduates.

Through flight school or the military, you learn the essentials of aviation—the theory of flight, which involves physics and mathematics; meteorology, which is the study of weather; and aircraft systems, which are the principles of how planes work. You must know how the parts of an aircraft operate—the engine, electrical system, and hydraulics. This training is essential when something goes wrong and you need to figure out how to fix things.

Navigation is another important subject. You have to understand how to read navigational charts to find your way across the world's airways. Geography helps as well, as you may need to use visual landmarks to guide your way. A little medical background is also required to be prepared in case a passenger or crew member becomes ill. On top of all this, pilots need to study the rules of flying set out by the Federal Aviation Administration. It's a lot to learn, but bringing together all these worlds of knowledge and applying them to a career can be exciting.

Solid work experience is another part of the climb to becoming a commercial pilot. Many future commercial pilots build hours as an instructor, and then take a job flying with small regional fleets and on corporate jets before advancing to the national airlines.

Once you do land this job, you will still need to pass a flight test every six months and keep up with the latest technology and procedures. Those tests are a long way off for you now. So at this point in your life, you can start exploring by reading about flying, visiting flight museums, and maybe building a model airplane or two. If you're serious about this career, talk to an actual pilot. Nobody can explain the job better than a family friend or relative who actually flies the friendly skies.

CHECK IT OUT

Young people interested in flying can learn more with young friends who also want to fly. Aviation Career Education camps bring middle and high school students together to learn about aviation history and the physics of flight, take field trips to aviation sites, and explore aviation through hands-on activities. To find a camp in your state, visit the Federal Aviation Administration's Web site at http://www.faa.gov and click on the education section.

CHAPTER 5

The Sky's the Limit

While a pilot may be the first job that jumps to mind when you think of careers in aviation, many other people are working together to keep the world's planes in the air. See if any of these jobs better suits your talents and interests.

Aerodynamics Engineer

These engineers are part of the team that helps build planes that fly more smoothly, efficiently, and quietly. Drawing on their knowledge of aerospace engineering, they use sophisticated computer programs to help create new plane designs. From their plans, they build scale models of planes and test them in wind tunnels so they can observe how the craft will react under simulated wind conditions. Computer programs called computational fluid simulations predict how different airplane shapes will perform. Most aerodynamics engineers have at least a bachelor's degree in engineering.

Aircraft Mechanic

These professionals are just like the mechanics who do car repair except they work on airplanes instead. They make sure

> ## "That big plane in front of the hangar is only as good as the man who flies it, and he is only as good as the people on the ground who work with him."
> —W. A. (PAT) PATTERSON, PRESIDENT OF UNITED AIRLINES

planes are safe to fly after each flight. They conduct extensive annual inspections every year. If an aircraft isn't operating correctly they get in "under the hood" and examine the engine and other mechanical parts to find the problem. Using hand and electric tools, they often replace faulty parts and repair the aircraft.

Some airline employees prefer to keep their feet on the ground.

ON THE JOB

NAME: Alfred Yoder
OFFICIAL TITLE: Director of Maintenance

What do you do?

I work as an aircraft mechanic for students and for customers who own their own planes. I work on the whole spectrum of privately owned airplanes from small single engines to large twins and corporate jets, but not commercial airplanes. Anything that goes wrong with an airplane, I take care of it. I'll fix an engine not running correctly or not getting enough power. I perform the annual inspection to make sure a plane is legal.

We have a whole list of things that we need to look at. Does the plane have the power it needs? Does it have oil pressure? Are all the temperatures correct? We go through step-by-step to see that the plane performs in the manner it was designed for. I like the satisfaction of being able to repair something and knowing that somebody is depending on me to supply a good, safe product. Something about troubleshooting a system that is very difficult—chasing the problem until it is repaired—is rewarding.

How did you get started?

I began cleaning bellies of airplanes. Then I proved myself helping an aircraft mechanic. I worked on twins and singles and really learned it. You get a license as an airplane mechanic after a year's study and then passing a written and practical test. It's good to get the education with the practical experience. If you work around airplanes a while and then get some schooling, it makes a lot more sense. There's always a need for more mechanics—especially those with good character, a work ethic, and common sense.

Airport Designer

Runways, terminals, towers, parking lots, roads, bridges—just think of all the elements that go into building an airport. Airport designers put all these elements together to make airports that operate efficiently and safely. They draw on their knowledge of architecture, construction, and civil engineering. (Civil engineers plan all the structures in areas that are used by the general public.) If you have seen a miniature model of an airport, that's exactly how airport designers visualize how to put together the elements of a new airport.

Airport Manager

Just as a fast food restaurant or department store has a manager, so do airports. Managers oversee all the operations at the airport and report directly to the private owners or to the local government authorities. Most airport managers excel at handling staff, business matters, public relations, accounting, civil engineering (for construction at the airport), and politics. Think of all the restaurants and shops in an airport. Managers take care of renting those spaces. If a new runway has to be built, they consider how to best construct it and at what cost. Business and management experience is the key to this job.

Air Traffic Controller

From the airport control tower, the air traffic controller directs all flight activities, gives advice and information by radio to pilots, and monitors planes in and around the airport. It's a job that takes great coordination, mental alertness, and clear communication skills.

Aviation Psychologist

This may be a very narrow field but it's an interesting one. Employed by various government, academic, and private institutions, aviation psychologists study pilot performance and how to reduce flight crew error. Because pilots depend on fast, clear information, psychologists often focus on how details about the weather and possible hazards reach a pilot and how that information is conveyed to the copilot and cabin attendants. Studies by psychologists can lead to the design of improved equipment and systems for human interaction.

Copilot

The copilot is one of two pilots who usually make up the cockpit crew and they work as a close team. Copilots, often called first officers, are second in command on a plane, and they share duties with the captain or main pilot. They operate specific flight controls and carefully watch gauges and controls and keep logs. They often take care of radio communications with air traffic controllers and track weather conditions as a flight progresses. The copilot generally has less experience than the pilot, but like an understudy in acting or a relief pitcher, she or he steps in to safely fly the plane if a pilot can't perform his or her duties. On many international flights there are two first officers, primarily because the flights are so long and they can give each other a chance to rest.

Design Engineer

If you've ever made a paper or model airplane, you've dabbled in airplane design. Professional airplane designers do the same thing but on a much larger scale. The world's largest commercial airliners designed so far are the Boeing 747, which typically carry about 400 people, and the new AirBus A380, which is created to hold as many as 850 passengers. Depending on the type of plane needed, a designer decides how long a plane will be, how many

Keeping aircraft in tip-top shape is a top priority.

NAME: Maria Heins

OFFICIAL TITLE: Flight Instructor

What do you do?

I'm 19 and I teach people from ages 16 to 55 to fly. I have five students I work with now on a weekly basis. I start by going over how an airplane flies and the requirements for getting a pilot's license. Normally, what we do is break a lesson up into an hour on the ground and about two hours in flight. The airplane has dual controls so I can control the plane when needed.

It takes full-time students about three months to get a license. I love the challenge and sense of accomplishment that I see in my students as they work toward their solo flight. It's amazing.

How did you get started?

I started getting interested in flying when I was babysitting for a lady when I was 13 back in Spokane, Washington. She was becoming a flight instructor, and she practiced teaching the ground lessons with my sister and me. After she took me flying in a small Cessna 172, I was totally hooked. I absolutely loved it.

So I went to a little flight school next and asked to volunteer. I washed planes and did paperwork in exchange for flight lessons. On my 16th birthday I had enough lessons to fly solo. When I was 17, I got my private pilot's license. I couldn't see myself working in an office so when I got out of high school, I looked into flight school.

I came to the school here in Arizona for a program that takes you all the way through to getting your commercial license.

ON THE JOB

A lot of people become instructors as a transition job—it's good experience and a lot of fun. Then people often go on to the airlines. I have a job starting soon flying cargo out of Columbus, Ohio, on a 40-foot-long transport plane. Eventually, I think I'd like to live overseas and maybe fly for medical relief work, taking supplies where they are needed.

I started getting interested in flying when I was babysitting for a lady when I was 13...

NAME: Trevor Williams
OFFICIAL TITLE: Flight Attendant

What do you do?

I ensure the comfort and safety of customers. People see us do the safety demonstrations but they don't think how we are really there mostly for safety. We go through a five-week course of training on all different types of safety things, including medical and emergency evacuation procedures. On my last flight, I had a guy who passed out. We had to get him a little oxygen and take his blood pressure. I go through recurrent annual training to relearn some customer service skills and some medical procedures. You have to know how to go down those slides for an emergency landing. You go through drills in a simulator. You have to get the people out in 90 seconds.

ON THE JOB

People management is key for me. You have to deal with tons of baggage and getting seats upright and giving out the food. You interact with so many different people every day on a plane—I really love that. You run across so many different kinds of behavior—good and bad.

I get to the airport early to prepare for flights. I have a briefing with my ground agents to discuss when they will send the passengers on and other things. Customer service personnel come on the plane and ask what we need—pillows, provisions, ice, etc. When we first get on a plane we do a safety check of all our safety equipment. We also go over the flight plan with the pilot and discuss what the weather and how long the flight will be.

How did you get started?

I was working in banking and I had several friends who were flight attendants and enjoyed it. The flexibility of the schedule attracted me. Every month you have control of your schedule. You have to work a minimum of 70 hours per month to be full time. I do 120 hours a month and I'm still able to keep about 15 days off. That's flexibility.

I'm working on my master's degree in corporate finance at the same time. It's also a great way to see the world. I will work three flights soon and then wind up in Ft. Lauderdale for 26 hours, so I will get some beach time in. The airline pays for the hotel and I get a daily food allowance while I'm away. That's one of the cool things.

people or cargo items it will hold, how wide it will be, where the wings should be placed, and how strong the materials need to be. These professionals usually have at least a college degree in mechanical, civil, or aerospace engineering.

Equipment Engineer

If you've flown on a major airline, you know that it can some-times get hot and stuffy. That's when you reach up and turn the knob in the ceiling to point the airflow directly at you. This type of air conditioning and circulation system is created by an equip-ment engineer. These specialists focus on building the mechanical and electrical elements of a plane, including systems for heating, pressurizing, hydraulics, and/or oxygen equipment. Equipment engineers usually need an educational background in mechani-cal, electrical, or systems engineering.

Federal Air Marshal

If police work and aviation appeal to you, you might consider this career. These specialized agents protect passengers and crew in the event of a plane hijacking. Air Marshals disguise themselves as ordinary travelers to blend in with passengers aboard high-risk routes worldwide. Marshals can carry firearms on planes and make arrests without warrants. While you have to be on the lookout for trouble all the time, it can also be a tedious job because most flights are uneventful. It's not surprising that you have to complete strict psychological testing and training to get into this line of work. Because of limited funding, there are only enough marshals to protect fewer than 5 percent of daily U.S. flights. Check the Transportation Security Administration (TSA) Web site for more info at http://www.tsa.gov.

Flight Attendant

You might first think of flight attendants as glorified waiters in the sky. While it's true they do serve food to passengers and tend to their other requests, a flight attendant's number-one concern is safety. He or she is prepared to assist passengers in emergencies, whether there is plane trouble or a customer suffers a sudden ill-ness. Most attendants work only part time and earn enough to pursue other interests.

Flight Dispatcher

Every flight is tracked by a Federal Aviation Administration dispatcher on the ground. The flight dispatchers work with the pilots planning flight details like fuel consumption, altitudes, traffic flow, and weather. To plan the best routes, dispatchers consider winds aloft and look for the best tailwinds or the least headwinds. They authorize takeoffs or cancel flights. They often work under pressure in a noisy, hectic office with other airport workers. They rely on computers, calculators, and weather charts—sometimes doing the job of a meteorologist. Most of these positions require a college degree with a major in air transportation and some background in meteorology.

Flight Instructor

This might be one of the scariest aviation careers because you have to sit next to someone who has no experience flying and let that person take control of the aircraft. Actually, the dual controls in a teaching plane make flying safe. Instructors also teach students on the ground in the classroom and in flight simulators. Many pilots start out as instructors because it's a good way to gain the experience and hours needed to advance.

Flight Operations Director

The flight operations director coordinates all of the flying activity at an airport or test facility. He or she oversees the flying, training, and maintenance schedules for the pilots and airplanes. When a pilot is scheduled for a check flight to make sure a repaired plane is operating correctly, the director arranges the schedule and assigns a pilot to the job.

Meteorologist

Weather can be a pilot's best friend or biggest enemy. The pilot relies on a meteorologist to know what to expect during a flight and map the best course possible. If conditions are too windy, snowy, or foggy, pilots get that info from a meteorologist. This expert analyzes weather data and makes weather reports to the pilot and dispatcher and then works with the flight dispatcher preparing flight plans. A college level bachelor's degree in meteorology is required for this job.

NAME: Chuck Adams

OFFICIAL TITLE: Air Traffic Controller

What do you do?

I guide planes in and out of the airport. I make sure pilots know they're on the right runway, I make sure pilots understand what approach they're supposed to fly into the airport on, and I make sure the weather information is up-to-date and accurate. And I can often see all the planes from the tower. When you work radar you often don't get to see all that.

Different air traffic controllers handle different parts of each flight. A ground traffic controller talks to an aircraft as it moves away from the gate. Then, when the aircraft gets close to the runway, the pilot switches frequencies and talks to another controller in the control tower. That controller makes sure that there are no conflicts in the air so that that plane can safely fly. The next controller is departure control and he takes the plane up to 10,000 to 15,000 feet and then hands the aircraft off to another air traffic controller who is typically located in one of the big centers around the country. Then when you start to land the process reverses.

Here at Grand Forks we have a lot of student and corporate travel. We're a 24-hour facility. I suppose we do roughly 285,000 operations a year—that's about 700 to 800 flights average per day. Our busiest day was about 2,200 aircraft. There are so many planes coming in and out that you have to be able to multitask. There are hundreds of lives in my hands at any one time. You also have to be a clear communicator. You have to make sure your speech is clear. Microphone or "mic" fright can be one of the biggest barriers to doing this job.

How did you get started?

I got a lot of my technical training in the Air Force and I worked at several different places around the world and got experience as an air traffic controller. I'm not trained as a pilot and you don't need a pilot background to get into this, but it certainly could help. Colleges offer courses now in air traffic control. Even when you study it at college you gain experience working in a simulated tower with a console with a screen that wraps around you so you feel like you're actually working with aircraft.

ON THE JOB

This Is Your Pilot Speaking

Match the aviation term with its meaning.

A Crash pad

B Deadheading

C Puddle jumper

D Dogfight

E Barnstormer

F Domicile

1 Daring stunt pilot from the early days of aviation

2 The city where a pilot is based and where his or her trips begin and end

3 Aerial battle between enemy planes during wartime

4 When a pilot travels to work on an aircraft that he or she isn't flying

5 An apartment or house where pilots stay when they're away from home—usually shared by several pilots.

6 Small commuter plane equipped for water landings

POP QUIZ

ANSWERS: A-5, B-4, C-6, D-2, E-1, F-2

Security Staff

Before you board a plane, you have to go through security checkpoints and have your carry-on bags X-rayed and searched by screeners who are making sure nothing dangerous or illegal goes aboard. Screeners also make passengers walk through metal detectors to make sure they are not bringing any harmful items onboard. For extra security, they physically search people at random. Security people are really the first line of defense against possible acts of terrorism, and their jobs have become more important as acts of terrorism have increased. As they enforce airport regulations and patrol the grounds, they keep a watchful eye for any suspicious, unattended bags. They must be super alert for potential dangers. To identify themselves as security, they must wear badges and usually clothes with "TSA" clearly printed on them. TSA stands for Transportation Security Administration, the federal government agency that employs the screeners. Security candidates undergo extensive background checks to make sure they are reliable and trustworthy. Check out the TSA Web site at http://www.tsa.gov.

Ticket Agent

The first friendly face you see upon entering the airport is often the ticket agent. They officially check passengers in at the airport—making sure they have seat assignments and proper identification. Agents also sell tickets, weigh and tag luggage, and answer questions on schedules and fares. You need good communication skills for this job and the ability to handle passengers' complaints and frustrations. It's a job that can take great patience, and you can usually start out with just a high school degree.

CHAPTER 6

Kids Ask, Pilots Answer

To find out what kids really want to know about being a pilot, we went to the source and asked real middle school students from Washington and California for questions they would ask real commercial airline pilots. We posed their questions to Colleen Andersen-Briscoe, a pilot with United Airlines, and Robert Bates, a pilot with Continental Airlines.

When did you start flying and how did you get interested in flying?

—Tom M., age 11

Colleen: I started flying right after graduation from high school. My parents were both employees of major airlines. My sister and I got to travel a lot as children, using our parents' travel benefits. When I traveled as a little girl, it never entered my mind that women could be airline pilots. On airplanes then, "wings" were handed out by stewardesses (now called flight attendants) to children. The boys always got "Future Pilot" wings and the girls were given "Future Stewardess" pins. By the time I was 17, I knew that I wanted to do something that not every other woman was doing. I started seriously thinking about what it would take to become an airline pilot.

"Going to college is an important step to becoming a commercial airline pilot."

—COLLEEN ANDERSEN-BRISCOE

I went to the career center in my high school and researched what kind of educational requirements and training it would take to reach my goal. First I had to find out if I would even like flying a small airplane. I remember paying $25 for a 30-minute introductory flight at the local airport. As we accelerated down the runway, he let me follow through on the controls. As soon as we lifted off, and I could see the ground below me, I knew that I was hooked on flying and wanted to become a pilot.

Robert: I grew up on a farm and enjoyed operating trucks and tractors. I thought about flying once I started driving. When I received some money from my grandmother, I took my first flying lessons while in college and got my private pilot's license.

What school did you go to and how did you train to be a pilot?

–Katy W., age 11

Colleen: I went to San Jose State University for its aeronautics program, which gave me airplane knowledge combined with business courses. I learned to fly at San Carlos Airport,

EMERGENCY EXIT
PUSH WINDOW AND PULL RELEASE

Robert Bates

just south of San Francisco International Airport. When I graduated college, I worked as a certified flight instructor for one year to build up my flying hours. Then I joined the Coast Guard and worked as a reservist on active duty for five and a half years before getting a job as an airline pilot.

Robert: I learned to fly in Colorado, while attending Colorado University in Boulder. After college, I worked in business for a year and then decided to apply to become an officer in the military. I was accepted to Navy Aviation Officer Candidate School. I did two years of Navy pilot training and then four years more active duty full time. I resigned from the Navy to pursue an airline career, but I have stayed in the Navy Reserves on a part-time basis. I built my flight experience flying freight, and then was hired by Continental as a passenger pilot. I currently fly B-737s for both Continental and the Navy.

Do you need to go to college to become a commercial pilot?

—Raenna R., age 13

Colleen: Going to college is an important step to becoming a commercial airline pilot. In fact, a bachelor's degree is usually a requirement, but it can be in any subject really—there are English majors who make great pilots.

Robert: There's no requirement by the FAA to have college experience to fly commercially, but the military and most major airlines require a degree.

Is it difficult to fly a plane?

—Nicholas R., age 11

Colleen: It's not necessarily difficult to fly a plane, but it takes lots of practice to learn the skills to be a proficient and safe pilot. The highest level of attention you need is during takeoff and landing. You're flying closer to the ground, and you have more airplane traffic around you, so you have more checklists to run. There's a lot to think about.

Robert: It's not difficult—it just takes building blocks. You start with lots of ground school and understanding of weather, aerodynamics, physics, etc., and then learn to fly a small plane. Then you can fly larger planes, with more complicated systems and multiengines. Then you're ready to learn how to fly jets, which move faster and require faster planning and skills. Eventually, you learn to fly big, complicated airliners. Sometimes the weather is bad or visibility is bad or the runway is icy. Generally, the weather can make flying somewhat difficult.

Do you get nervous when you get turbulence?

—Nicholas R., age 11

Colleen: Sometimes turbulence can be a bit unnerving, but I always have confidence in knowing that airplanes are built to withstand turbulence. My main concern is keeping the flight attendants and passengers safe. A lot of people don't understand it so it scares them.

Robert: Sometimes it can get pretty bad—pretty bumpy. No aircraft has run into any real trouble because of turbulence, but people have been hurt in the cabin. It's unstable air. It has a *sheer*, which means some of the air is moving up while some of the air is moving down. Or some is moving left while some is moving right. Sheer causes the plane to shake. We usually try to fly over turbulence and bad weather.

How do you deal with the responsibility of flying so many people in the plane?

—Raenna R., age 13

Colleen: It's a lot of responsibility and I always take it very seriously. My philosophy has always been that if I keep myself safe in the cockpit or flight deck, then everyone seated behind me will be safe, too. Pilots receive lots of training to keep their skills sharp, so that we can handle everyday duties, as well as the rare emergency.

Robert: At first it's daunting, but after a year or two you don't really think about it. You think about it as exercising the training you've received and that you're following the procedures to ensure the flight is a safe one.

What do you like about being a pilot?

—Claire M., age 8

Colleen: There is something special about seeing the earth from a vantage point several miles above. I get to see spectacular sunrises and sunsets and other phenomenal sights. I get to see the Northern lights, lightning in a thunderstorm, and St. Elmo's Fire, which is like sparks on the front windshield. Or I may see the sunrise twice in one day. I get to travel and meet lots of people. Every flight is different from the last one.

Robert: The flying can be mundane because the autopilot can do so much of the flying. The exciting part is the first half hour and the last half hour of every flight—that's the takeoff and climbing through the clouds. It can be raining at the airport, but when you climb through the clouds it's always sunny on top. Then when you plan your descent from 40,000 feet, nearly eight miles up in the sky, and get the plane lined up. You bring it down hopefully smoothly. That's a great part of the job.

How many states have you flown to and how many airports have you been to?

—Griffin L., age 11

Colleen: I've flown to about 35 states in the U.S. and to 17 countries. I've been as far north as Fairbanks, Alaska, and far away as New Delhi, India. I've also flown to well over 110 airports as an airline pilot.

Robert: I think I've been to every state in the country and many, many airports. I've probably been to every country in Western Europe and to several in Asia and Africa. It's great to go to a new place. I was

Griffin L.

in Gulfport, Mississippi, the other day and you might not think that's a great place to visit, but it was fantastic.

Is it fun to fly a plane?

–Natalie R., age 8

Colleen: Overall, it is fun to fly a plane. Knowing that you are in command of a complex airplane can be exhilarating.

Robert: Flying little planes is more fun than big planes. Flying fighter jets is fun—I did some training landing on aircraft carriers. An airliner is not as exciting as some other planes.

Jacob T. (and Cheryl)

Tell me about a time you were nervous flying and what's the scariest thing that ever happened to you while you were flying?

–Jacob T., age 11

Colleen: As a student pilot, I was required to fly several "solo" cross-country flights in preparation for my private pilot certificate. On one particular flight, I was navigating by dead reckoning (course, distance, time). When I got to my destination airport, things didn't look quite right because of the haze, so I was nervous. I contacted the tower controllers. I was surprised to find out that I was about 10 miles south of the airport I really wanted to land at. You have to fess up when you've made a mistake and ask for help.

Robert: The only time I've been nervous recently was because of a very unusual aircraft systems problem involving the landing gear. On this flight, we put the gear handle down in the cockpit and normally that lowers all the landing gear and gets the plane ready to land. But one of the landing gears wasn't going down all the way. That makes it difficult to land. Fortunately, there is an emergency procedure you can perform in the cockpit that can help solve the problem. We did that and it worked.

CHAPTER 7

Virtual Apprentice
PILOT FOR A DAY

Check your instruments—it's time to take the *Virtual Apprentice* challenge and be a pilot for a day. Here's a "flight plan" you can navigate through on your own, or ask your teacher to make this an all-class activity to celebrate the first century of modern aviation.

8:00 Pilots spend a lot of work hours filling out checklists to make sure no detail related to a flight gets overlooked. Create a checklist of all the assignments included for each hour in your Virtual Apprentice experience and check off each one as you complete it.

9:00 Learn firsthand about the mechanics of flight by designing and constructing your own airplane. Use paper, scissors, paper clips, and tape to build your plane. In class, divide into small teams to complete this project.

10:00 Every aircraft has its own unique tail number (actually a combination of letters and numbers) that serves to identify it, like the serial number on a car. Give your flyer a tail number and then test-fly it both inside and outdoors, if possible. Make any necessary adjustments to improve your plane's performance. Then compete against other models to find the best design.

11:00 Pilots today train on flight simulators (virtual versions of what pilots experience at the controls of different planes) as well as in actual aircraft. Computerized flight simulations are a lot like video games, but as a pilot once said, "Flying is not Nintendo. You don't push a button and start over." Find a free flight simulator to download into your computer at Thirty Thousand Feet Aviation Directory http://www.thirtythousandfeet.com/flightsi.htm.

12:00 Take a lunch break. A hungry pilot is a distracted pilot. Be sure to eat a healthy lunch, too—it's hard to squeeze into the left seat (that's where the pilot always sits) when there's a lot of junk in your trunk!

1:00 Since some letters sound the same over the radio, pilots and air traffic controllers use the Aviation Alphabet to make sure they come across loud and clear. Learn this alphabet, and you'll be a step ahead in flight school: A=Alpha, B=Bravo, C=Charley, D=Delta, E=Echo, F=Foxtrot, G=Golf, H=Hotel, I=India, J=Juliet, K=Kilo, L=Lima, M=Mike, N=November, O=Oscar, P=Papa, Q=Quebec, R=Romeo, S=Sierra, T=Tango, U=Uniform, V=Victor, W=Whiskey, X=X-Ray, Y=Yankee, Z=Zulu. Practice saying your own name, then try saying a friend's name. Write a short sentence using the Aviation Alphabet. See if your classmates can understand what you're saying.

2:00 Search in the library or on the Web using the keywords *aviation history* to learn five fun facts about the history of this field. If you're working as a class, share your discoveries with the other students.

3:00 Fast forward to the bicentennial of flight in the year 2103—write a page describing what YOU think the pilots of the future will need to know or draw a picture of the kinds of aircraft they will fly.

4:00 Grab a pencil and paper and head outdoors for some plane spotting. Notice where the flight paths are near your house and choose a busy patch of sky to watch for **45** minutes. Record the number and types of aircraft you see during that time (passenger or cargo jet, float plane, helicopter, small private plane, military aircraft, etc.) as well as any other details you notice (colors, decorations, or other identifying marks on the plane). If you have binoculars or live close to an airport, you may even be able to identify the particular airline each plane belongs to.

5:00 Pack a hearty meal, squeeze into a small closet, and stay there for 33 1/2 hours (just kidding!). If you can stay awake the whole time you're in there, you'll have an idea of what Charles Lindbergh experienced during his solo flight across the Atlantic. (Or, better yet, you could just read *The Spirit of St. Louis* by Charles Lindbergh and hear from the pilot himself what that famous flight was like.)

Virtual Apprentice
PILOT FOR A DAY: FIELD REPORT

If this is your book, use the space below to jot down a few notes about your Virtual Apprentice Experience (or use a blank sheet of paper if this book doesn't belong to you). What did you do? What was it like? How did you do with each activity? Don't be stingy with the details!

8:00 VIRTUAL APPRENTICE CHECKLIST: _____
_____
_____
_____

9:00 PAPER AIRPLANE: _____
_____
_____
_____

10:00 TEST FLIGHT: _____
_____
_____
_____

11:00 FLIGHT SIMULATION: _____
_____
_____
_____

12:00 LUNCH: _____

_____

_____

1:00 AVIATION ALPHABET: _____

_____

_____

_____

2:00 AVIATION HISTORY: _____

_____

_____

_____

3:00 PILOT OF THE FUTURE: _____

_____

_____

_____

4:00 PLANE WATCH: _____

_____

_____

_____

5:00 SOLO FLIGHT: _____

_____

_____

_____

Count Me In (or Out)

DO YOU HAVE THE RIGHT STUFF?

The following activities may help determine how you'll meet the challenges you'll face on the way to becoming a pilot. Write your answers on a separate piece of paper and refer back to them when you reach your cruising altitude.

Which statement best describes how you feel about flying?

❏ The air is my natural element—ever since I was a little kid I've had my head in the clouds. I won't be happy until I have earned my pilot's license and can take to the friendly skies.

❏ The last time I flew on an airplane, the air stank of peanuts, my legs fell asleep, and it seemed like the turbulence would never end.

❏ I'd rather keep my feet on solid ground. Other jobs in aviation that interest me are:

_____

_____

_____

_____

_____

_____

When I'm at an airport, I spend more time:

❏ Buying breath mints.

❏ Checking for change in pay phones.

❏ Watching the planes as they take off and land.

❏ Searching for my boarding pass, which I probably left in the bathroom.

The idea of being a pilot:

❏ Thrills me to no end. I can't wait to get into a cockpit and start messing with all those cool gadgets!

❏ Scares me half to death. Who do you ask for directions if you get lost up there in the wild, blue yonder?

❏ Makes me wonder if maybe it might just be possible that some day an airline will trust me behind the wheel of a multi-billion-dollar jet loaded with hundreds of passengers.

When you hear the word "cockpit," you immediately think:

❏ Technology! Bring it on!

❏ Claustrophobia! Get me out of there!

Aviation is an amazing field with a fascinating history. The pilots of the past didn't have computers to help them—they had to rely primarily on their flying skills...and sheer guts! Some famous aviators that I'd definitely like to learn more about are:

_____

_____

_____

_____

I'll leave the flying to the pilots—an airplane cockpit is too small a space for all my BIG ideas. My interests in aerodynamics and engineering will help me design and build the next generation of flying machines. The three words that I think best describe the future of aviation are:

_____

_____

_____

_____

_____

APPENDIX

More Resources for Young Pilots

BOOKS

There are a bazillion great books about careers in aviation and the fascinating history of flight. Here are a few that get high marks:

Bledsoe, Karen and Glen. *Airplane Adventures*. Mankato, Minn.: Capstone Press, 2001.

Hansen, Ole Steen. *Amazing Flights: The Golden Age*. New York: Crabtree Publishing, 2003.

Pasternak, Ceel and Linda Thornburg. *Cool Careers for Girls in Air and Space*. Manassas Park, Va.: Impact Publications, 2001.

Zaunders, Bo. *Feathers, Flaps, & Flops: Fabulous Early Fliers*. New York: Dutton, 2001.

Graham, Ian. *Flight*. New York: Kingfisher, 2001.

Hart, Phillip. *Flying Free: America's First Black Aviator*s. Minneapolis, Minn.: Lerner Publications, 1996.

PROFESSIONAL ASSOCIATIONS

Experimental Aircraft Association (EAA) Young Eagles Program
P.O. Box 3086
Oshkosh, Wisconsin 54903-3086
http://www.eaa.org

FAA (Federal Aviation Administration)
800 Independence Ave. SW
Washington, D.C. 20591
http://www.faa.gov

International Society of Women Airline Pilots
http://www.iswap.org

International Young Aeronauts
http://www.iya-online.org

NASA (National Air and Space Administration)
Suite 5K39
Washington, D.C. 20546-0001
http://www.nasa.gov

WEB SITES

NASA has lots of good sites, including:
http://eto.nasa.gov

If you'd like to know more about aeronautics, careers in aviation, and anything else you're curious about, the How Stuff Works site has loads of fascinating information at http://www.howstuff works.com.

Kids' Fly Zone at http://www.centennialofflight.gov/user/kids .htm

Learn about the history of airmail at this great interactive site: http://www.historicwings.com/features99/airmail

The Thirty Thousand Feet aviation directory provides tons of links to Web sites for young aviators at http://www.thirtythou sandfeet.com/youth.htm.

INDEX